CHESS OPENINGS

A QUICKSTART GUIDE TO THE BEST OPENING STYLES, TACTICS, AND STRATEGIES TO WIN EVERY GAME

TABLE OF CONTENTS

INTRODUCTION

The records of the Chess term have been in life for quite a long time. Chess began from the start. Over the years, it turns out to be a complex recreation wherein many competitions spend productive time. It has said Chess was created in India. Chaturanga, the ancient game, turned into a game around the 6th century in northwestern India. These 4 gadgets represented 4 different sorts of military devices. The corporations had been infantry, elephants, cavalry, and chariots.

Chess was inaugurated to Europeans around a thousand AD. At that time, the Queen, named Vizier, had the simplest movement of Kings. The Queen was not able to move except with the gap in it. The Queen would turn out to be the most important piece, and Chess is known as the "Queen's Chess."

As you might already know, Chess is a board game where everything is built on strategy. It is a highly competitive game that is played between two players. But people also play Chess as a part of their recreation. One of the very important things about a game and in this is the opening, and that is what this book is about. Before we go into such details, let me give you a brief introduction to chess.

If you are looking for a book that is easy to understand and will provide you with practical tips that will help you win a game, and then you are at the right place because this book has it all.

If you want to train yourself and learn the game like an expert, then you need two very important things — the first thing is to open your mind and allow thoughts to wander freely, and the second thing is discipline. This book is going to help you inculcate both these things. Firstly, it has tons of information about different types of openings that you should know about, and it also has a great deal of advice regarding those individual openings. Moreover, you will also get endless suggestions inside this book that will all help you to brush up on your tactics and always stay one step ahead of your opponent.

There are so many chess openings possible in the world that it is not possible for any single book to cover them all in a comprehensive manner, and so, in this book, I have tried to include all the important openings. I have made sure that there are openings to suit everyone's style of play and also every difficulty level. It doesn't matter whether you are just a beginner, an intermediate, or an expert. This book is meant for everyone. You are also going to learn about some general principles that every player should know before they start strategizing their openings.

In this book, we are solely going to focus on the opening where your main aim is to mobilize your pieces in the most efficient manner possible. The two main things that define any opening are the piece placements and pawn structures. When you are a beginner, you might feel that the pawns are weak and do not hold any power at all, but the more you play, the more you will realize that they do hold a lot of power. You simply have to know how to wield it.

Even though from the outside, it may seem that there are million different possibilities from a chess opening, at its very core, the fundamental characteristics of any opening remain the same. These characteristics are kind, safety, pawn structure, material, space, and time.

Development is a key part of any opening. It is the development that denotes the time factor in a chess opening. Many people think that development means the pace at which you are playing the game, but that's wrong. It refers to how fast you are putting all your forces at work. Whenever you make a move, your opponent gets their turn to make a move in turn.

In this book, I will explain why opening strategies are so critical and why standard openings just don't work anymore.

The importance of opening strategies is something that many professional chess players know about, most often through experience. However, the majority of real-life players tend to rely on "standard" opening moves. These are moves that they have been told and drilled over and over until they are memorized and can perform flawlessly. They are boring to watch and often contain traps, but "standard" openings can win games.

If you follow this guide, you will understand the game in-depth. We will provide you with gameplay graphics and relevant explanations to ensure that you get a better insight and start playing it right from the very first move.

If you think that focusing on your pieces and pawns is enough to ensure your win, then you are absolutely wrong. Observing enemy pieces and their moves is a crucial element in this game. Whites are always the first ones to make a move. So, in this guide, we will talk about some of the best opening moves you can make as Whites and also some best defending moves you can make as Blacks.

We will not only teach you some efficient opening sequences but will also enlighten you about why to use them and how to change them according to your unique gameplay.

This GUIDE on chess opening explores secret moves to always win every game with aggressive strategies and traps used by professionals. Chess opening should not be difficult.

Learn how to study EFFICIENT openings. Know what openings you ought to look at. Get practical and efficient opening advice, and don't worry about what to do at this stage!

With these openings, chess players learn how the chess piece moves in the real world. They learn the basic moves of all the pieces. They learn the openings of the squares at the beginning of the game. Therefore, chess players are able to learn the basic moves of the most basic chess piece in one of many ways.

A few thoughts in the opening are very deep or interesting and will be hard to translate by unadulterated calculation. Subsequently, get familiar with the well-known openings to stay away from traps and early bungles.

CHAPTER 1

Opening Principles

Controlling the Center

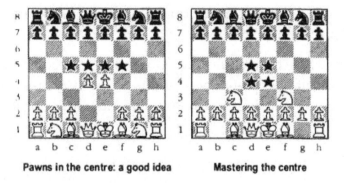

Pawns in the centre: a good idea   Mastering the centre

I n sports, the emphasis is often placed on the center — in football, the center of the field is an important section of it. If you lose the center, then you will find it hard to control the team. The same is applicable in chess — the center of the board is crucial.

Now, you would want to ask, why is the center so important? Well, the answer to that question shouldn't be hard for anyone to guess. A chess piece can reach a lot of squares on the board from the central position. So, if you control the center, it means you can exercise control over many squares.

1

One good way of ensuring that you control the center is to place your Pawns there. In the first diagram shown above, you can see the two White Pawns occupying the center position. Notice the stars on the fifth rank in the first diagram. What do the stars depict? It means that Black cannot move a piece to those squares because any piece that is moved there would be captured by one of the White Pawns on d4 and e4.

In the second diagram, you can see the amount of power that a Knight will assume when it occupies a central position. The two White Knights on d3 and f3 have carefully protected the squares with a star in the second diagram. If Black moves any piece to those starred squares, one of the White knights will capture the piece.

For you to understand the power that a piece has when at the center, if you place the Knights in the diagram above on a3 and h3, respectively, they will have less influence.

One of the goals of any good opening should be to gain control of the center squares of the board. We are mainly focusing on the d4, d5, e4, and e5 squares, although c4, c5, f4, and F5 are also important squares to consider as they help control those four most important squares. The classic approach to the opening is to occupy these squares directly with Pawns and support them with your pieces.

The more recent idea is to control the center indirectly with pieces, leaving Pawns in a safer position and developing slowly. For this book, we are going to be taking a look at classical approaches as they best illustrate the principles of controlling and developing the center quickly.

By controlling the middle of the board with our Pawns, we will not only gain space to develop our other pieces behind our Pawns but limit the mobility of our opponent, hopefully causing them to have to choose the less ideal place for their pieces to not fall behind in development.

Imagine for a moment you are White, and you have a Pawn on d4 and e4, and your opponent hasn't moved any piece yet. Can you see how your Pawns create a wall blocking Black's access to the center? White is attacking all of the Black's side central squares: c5, d5, e5, and f5. Now, if Black were to try to occupy any of those squares, White can either defends the attacked piece to keep up the wall or exchange whichever they prefer. The point is that White has the choice about what happens, and Black has to play within that understanding.

Now, in a real game, White doesn't get to move twice before Black does, only once, but the principle is the same. Because White has an ever so slight advantage by choosing the first move, he will always start the game with a small space advantage and time advantage (called a tempo) over Black.

As such, White usually starts to play with confidence, staking a claim to the middle immediately and challenging Black to find equality given White's inherent advantage. Black, on the other hand, hopes to prove that White has overextended himself and gain equality in the position by taking his share of the space and winning back some of the lost tempo if possible. It's time we take a look at the development and how to get our pieces moving effectively.

Rapid Development

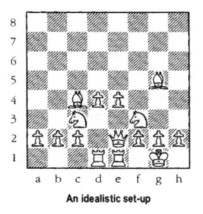

An idealistic set-up

In chess, development involves moving the most influential or valuable pieces like the Bishops, Knights, and Queen and using them to occupy the center position. You have to see those valuable pieces as your warriors — they won't have much power if you leave them at home. So, it is important that you send them into the field. Not just sending them into the field, you have to make sure that they occupy the central position. In the above diagram, you can see how White successfully developed his valuable pieces — by that move; White has secured the center for himself. White understands that it doesn't make sense for him to keep his valuable pieces at home while attacking with just a few. Even though the kind of setup in the diagram above will rarely play out in real life since the other opponent wouldn't let you, what you have to know is that it is important for you to develop your pieces rapidly early enough. Also, make sure you are using the pieces to occupy the central position. The arrangement doesn't necessarily have to be like the one in the sample diagram above.

King's Safety

White's king is safe

Remember fool's mate, which largely occurs due to negligence. So, when you are developing your pieces, it is important for you to consider the safety of your king. Both teams in a chess game usually move one of their knights to the center early enough. The developed Knight can easily be exchanged, leaving the center a bit porous.

Once you have castled, you will be sitting protected for a while so long as Pawns are blocking a direct path to you. Openings are very much influenced by the level of King´s safety. All Pawns covering the King are kept away from the openings, and the local area covered by the King is not left exposed. Also, in your opening, it is never advisable to shift your King from the first rank. If your King leaves the first rank as early as during openings, your chances of losing go very high.

It is not a good idea to leave your King in the central position when you have moved your Knight. A vicious attack along the central file can be brutal on your King. A good way to keep your King safe early enough is to castle as soon as you get the chance.

In the diagram shown above, the White King is castled with the White rook along the kingside. You can see the three pawns duly protecting the King from all attacks — that's a good way to guide your King.

Development

When it comes to developing pieces of Chess, it must be said: don't move the same piece twice without a good reason. It doesn't mean to pass up on great opportunities should they arise, nor neglect your defense if moving that piece is your best option. Generally speaking, you should aim to develop all your other pieces first before moving that same piece twice if you can help it. If anyone has ever told you that you shouldn't bring your Queen out early in Chess, this is one of the key reasons why.

The Queen is incredibly powerful and, as such, is also valuable. While it might be tempting to swing out his Queen for a dramatic check early, chances are you are leaving your opponent with a valuable target to attack while also developing his own pieces. If you have to spend time running away while your opponent is making moves with his pieces, that means you are falling behind. For these reasons, most people develop their minor pieces first (Knight and Bishop) and use their major pieces in supportive roles (Rook and Queen). A typical opening from White is e4.

This move is the start of many famous Chess lines and is fantastic for several reasons. First, this move directly stakes a claim on the center by giving White control of the d5 and f5 squares. If you remember, those are two of the center squares that are very important for the opening. Also, by moving the Pawn out of the way, it leaves White with several great options for turn 2. White has the option to develop either Knight to great squares in nc3 or for the queenside or nf3 and ne2 for the Kingside. White could instead choose to deploy his light-colored Bishop anywhere along the a6–f1 diagonal. Finally, there is still the option to move another Pawn, such as the popular King's Gambit. For Black, a typical response might be e4 c5.

The Sicilian Defense is a popular answer by Black to White's most common first move. This move stakes a claim in the center by occupying the c5 square and controlling the central d5 square White might have been looking otherwise. If you remember the position where White had a Pawn on both e4 and e5, it created a real block for Black to contend. This simple flanking Pawn maneuver gives Black control of that central square by stopping that d5 move from being played right away.

Additionally, this move gives the Black Knight a great square on c6 to occupy when it wants to. The c Pawn has already moved ahead, so the Knight won't have to worry about getting out of the way for a future Pawn advance. Another general principle in the opening is to castle early. We will touch on this topic more in King Safety, but your opening moves should generally work towards preparing you for the castle. By following these steps, you will be making successful moves.

Pawn Structure

Let's imagine that White has Pawns arranged on a2, b3, c4, d5, e5, f4, g3, and h2. These diagonal formations of Pawns are called Pawn Chains. Notice how each Pawn behind defends and supports the Pawn ahead of it. Pawn chains can be as small as two Pawns chained together in a diagonal. These are power formations to use to give the White a strong defensible position to play behind.

The next concept to consider with the Pawn structure is called Pawn Islands. Consider the same position as above but let's remove the c4 and f4 Pawns, meaning White has Pawns on a2, b3, d5, e5, g3, and h2. Do you notice how White's Pawns are separated into three separate groups? This means White now has three Pawn islands. In general, the more Pawn islands you have, the weaker your Pawns will be as they will be stretched thin and unable to defend one another.

An isolated Pawn is a single Pawn as an island with no Pawns on either side. Generally, isolated Pawns are considered a weak point in the defense as only pieces can ever defend them. There are always exceptions, but generally, isolated Pawns are something you hope to avoid.

Double Pawns or even triple Pawns can occur, which is just a fancy name given when two or even three Pawns end up on the same row. In most cases, these Pawns are considered a weakness as the Pawns on the same row cannot help protect each other.

Finally, a passed Pawn is a Pawn that no enemy Pawn can stop, as it has "passed" their attack range. In a position with White having a Pawn on e4, it would be a passed Pawn if no

Pawn on either the d or f file could stop it from advancing to promotion.

Open and Closed Positions

Open positions arise in openings where central Pawns are exchanged, and the center becomes more accessible. As the name suggests, these positions are filled with open spaces and long diagonals. As such, Rooks, Bishops, and the Queen all shine in these kinds of games, as they can best take advantage of the spaces. Closed games are ones where the Pawns are still on the board, usually locked in potential exchange, going many layers deep. These games are highly tactical and involve thinking many steps ahead in exchanges to determine who the potential victor would be in a big exchange in the middle. The theme of closed games is often maintaining the tension, as many times, the person who gives in to the pressure and attacks first comes out behind. In a closed position, Knights tend to shine a bit more as they are capable of maneuvering themselves around the tight battlefield better than most other pieces.

King Safety

If you develop pieces on both sides of the board before castling your King, you are opening yourself up to potentially devastating all-in attacks at very early turns in the game. The most extreme example of this is called the Fool's Mate, and it is the fastest way to lose a game of Chess. If you were curious: f3, e5, g4? Qh4.

However, it doesn't need to be as extreme as that to run into problems. Many exciting professional Chess matches were decided by gutsy sacrifice attacks made against a King stuck in the middle of the board. Such is Chess, but for beginners, it is always best to start by keeping the defense of your King in mind.

This ties into the last point on King safety, and that is the Pawns around your King. It is rarely a good idea to advance the three Pawns in the corner you want to castle unless you really have to. Any time you advance one of these Pawns, you are creating a tiny weakness in the defenses around your King that your opponent can later try to use to attack you.

Transposition

Many openings have similar elements and can be reached in different move orders. Being able to move from one opening into another is called Transposition and is one of the ways great players can stay flexible in their opening moves while sticking to the same overall opening plan. In response to your opponent's moves, it might be preferable to change your move order, but that doesn't mean you have to go off into unknown territory. Look for ways to transpose from your deviation back into a position you are familiar with. This is how the best players can play Chess in positions they are unfamiliar with. They make reasonable moves looking to go back into familiar territory.

CHAPTER 2

The First Move

Open Games

Double King Pawn or open games are openings for chess where the first movements are 1 e4 e5. They are by far the most popular two-way opening. It's famous because of its powerful movements. We will discuss in some detail these movements and the open game openings. Open games are classified in ECO C20–C99 codes.

Once E4 advance two squares of the White King's Pawn, in so doing, it fulfills various requirements of opening theory, center control, and rapid piece growth. Pawn claims to center and free the E2 square, clearing both the Bishop and the Queen a way to grow.

In comparison, move e4 weakens points, d4 and f4, and the pawn on e4 is still defenseless. By 2. By e5, Black produces White's place mirror image with the same advantages and drawbacks. We're in an open game now.

Now White has many second move options to choose from, and most of them are common.

The second is by far the most used NF3. This aims to connect the central e5 Pawn of Black, prepare for the Pawn to d4, build the Knight to its best square and clear a square of kingside castle, all of which comply with sound opening principles.

With 2 NF3

After two, Black also has some options, NF3. NF4. The most widely used is 2. NC6 defends and develops the pawn and center. If White plays 3 Bb5, the game will be opened by Ruy Lopez or Spanish. After two. The opening is called Scotch Game NC6 2. D4 and after 2. 3. NC6. BC4 is the game of Italy.

When Black plays 2. NF6, it's called Petrov's Defense rather than NC6, which preserves the mirror image. A second choice for Black is 2. D6 is beginning the defense of Philidor. Philidor Defense isn't common nowadays, even though it's a strong defense because it tends to limit Black mobility and initiative and give White more space. Not all other NF3 answers are suggested.

2 NF3 Alternatives

We are now considering White's second moves in an open game, legitimate alternatives. 2 NC3 starts the Game of Vienna, 2. BC4 leads to the Bishop's openings, and 2. F4 begins the King's Gambit.

The three openings listed lead to similar positions and the Bishop's opening to the same Vienna Game positions. This game usually involves the King's Gambit F4 advance to strike

14

the Black center. King's Gambit is built to quickly evolve and weaken the back center via a Bishop sacrifice.

The center game is another potential second move, 2. D4. This results in 2. EXD4 3. QXD4. EXD4 3. White would have a center open and a Queen formed prematurely. By playing the Danish Gambit two, he will stop the premature development of Queen. EXD4 3. C3 open center sacrificing Pawns.

These are the key openings of the open game. Napoleon opening (2. QF3), Parhama attack (2. QH5) and Portuguese opening (2. BB5), Konstantinopolsky opening (3. G3), Alapin's Opening (2. NE2), and Inverse Hungarian opening (4. BE2) are other opportunities for White to play in open games and are extremely dangerous and seldom encountered in master play except as experiments. Damiano Defense is regarded as extremely weak in the case of Black (2. F6), while Elephant Gambit (2. D5) and Latvian Gambit (2. F5) are considered to be highly risky.

Semi-Open Games

Semi-open games or single King awn games are chess openings where the White's first step is 2. E4 and any move other than symmetrical ones 2. E5. Some of the most famous Chess openings are included.

In semi-open openings in response to White's E4, which argues that White's Bishop and Queens have central squares and open lines, Black gives up every effort to create a mirror image by playing E5. Black will take some other routes instead. The philosophy and ideas behind each of these openings can be very different.

For example, the Sicilian Defense (1. C5) produces an unbalanced situation on the board, allowing both players to play with excellent opportunities and Black to take the initiative.

This explains the high popularity of this opening. In return for solidity, French Defense recognizes a certain lack of mobility. The first phase in the French Defense response is 1. E6, normally 2. D4 D5 follows.

There were 1. in Caro-Kann Defense. Move C6 normally is followed by 2. D4 D5 and Black use the C pawn to bolt the strong point on D5 and develop the Bishop on the queenside. In comparison, the Center Counter Defense, also called Scandinavian Defense (1. D5), calls for immediate tactical combat for the center.

Semi-open openings such as Alekhine's (1. NF6), Pirc (1. E4 D6 2. D4 NF6 3. NC3 G6), and Modern Defense (1. E4 G6) all operate under the theory of hyper-modern opening that allows White the formation of an extensive Black pawn's unimpeded center to attack it from a distance with parts.

The Nimzowitsch Defense and Owen Defense are other true semi-open openings. Nimzowitsch Defense (1. NC6) seeks to lead the game into dark lines that reject simple White goals. Owen's defense (1. B6) with an early Bishop enables White to develop a center and strike it from wings. In this opening, Black must be continuously cautious.

Sicilian Defense, closely followed by French Defense and Caro-Kann Defense, is the most common of semi-open openings in terms of popularity. There is also much exposure to Pirc Defense and Modern Defense, while Alekhine Defense and Scandinavian Defense play regularly.

Owen's Defense and Nimzowitsch Defense do not have many tournament plays during the legitimate semi-openings these days. Grob Defense (1. G5) and St. George Defense have experimental possibilities (1. A6).

The ECO codes are B20 to B99 for 1 E4 C5, Sicilian Defense, and B00 to B19 for 1. E4, preceded by every other move other than 1. C5, 1. E6, 1. E5.

Closed Games

The opening is called a close game or double Queen Pawn game if the first two movements of a chess match are 1. D4 D5. A significant thing to note about a closed game is that it does not automatically lead to closed positions. The word "closed" is simply a mark that does not represent the pieces.

Approach 1. D4 D5 provides similar benefits to approach 1. E4 E5. Both methods allow the player to manage the board's central squares, and both methods clear the path to a good opening for the Queen and the Bishop-two. However, the pawn is defenseless with the E4 opening, while the pawn has the advantage of being secured by the Queen with the opening D4.

This critical detail is part of the distinction between closed openings and other opening forms. This is why many Chess players prefer the Queen's Gambit (1. D4 D5 2. C4) to the King's Gambit (1. E4 E5 2. F4). Also, note that opening a closed game also becomes another form of opening, while opening a game does not.

CHAPTER 3

Greatest Chess Opening

The Queen's Gambit

Of all the closed openings, the Queen's Gambit openings are undoubtedly the favorite. It all starts with 2. C4 that offers the pawn. The opening then divides into variations based on how Black reacts. Note, this particular opening of the closed game is not a Gambit since the Pawn is still recovered.

The agreed Queen's Gambit happens when Black takes the Pawn with 2. DXC3. This capture is normally related to C5 and CXD5 movements later on. Black gives up possession of the central portion of the board to separate the White Pawn. White then should remain in charge of the centerboard and sustain the initiative by good workmanship.

On the other side, the Pawn offered can be ignored by Black. He can play 2. E6, producing Queen's Declined Gambit, or playing 2. C6 that produces Slav Defense — these openings have many variants, and every opening needs a lot of patience.

The following are only a couple of Queen's Declined Gambit variations: Lasker's Defense, Orthood Defense,

Cambridge Springs Defense, Tartakower Variation, Tarrasch Defense, and Semi-Tarrasch Defense.

Other less usual responses are the Chigorin Defense (2. NC6), Albin Countergambit (2. E5), the Symmetrical Defense (2. C5), the Baltic Defense (2. BF5), and the Marshall Defense framework (2. NF6). You won't ever see them, but certain masters like them.

The Reti Opening

This opening was named after grandmaster Richard Reti.

White plays Nf3 to open the game.

Black responds with d5.

White then plays c4, sacrificing his c4 pawn. If black chose to capture the pawn by playing dxc4, he would win a pawn but lose tempo by giving white a development advantage. This move would also damage black's pawn structure by doubling his pawns on the c file. White could follow up with Nc3, getting ahead in development.

Advantages (for White):

- Gives White early control of the E5 square, limiting Black's movements.

19

- Allows White to castle quickly.

Disadvantages (for White):

- Blocks the F-Pawn.

- Example: Fridrik Olafsson vs. David Bronstein, 1971

This game was played in Moscow, Russia, in 1971. Olafsson had White pieces, and Bronstein had Black pieces.

White (Olaffsson) opened the game by playing Nf3.

Black (Bronstein) responded with d5.

White then played c4, sacrificing his c pawn and attacking black's d5 pawn. Black could have responded with dxc4, but this would have doubled black's pawns on the c file. So instead, black played d4, maintaining a neat pawn structure.

White then played g3, preparing to fianchetto his light-squared bishop, and black played g6, preparing to fianchetto his dark-squared bishop.

White played Bg2, fianchettoing his light-squared bishop as planned and preparing to castle kingside. Black fianchettoed his dark-squared bishop by playing Bg7 as expected.

White continued with d3, defending his c4 pawn and opening a door for his dark-squared bishop to come into the game. Black played d5, adding a defender to his d4 pawn and gaining space on the board.

White castled kingside as planned and black played Ne7, developing his knight and preparing to castle kingside.

White continued with b4, gaining space on the queen side. Black castled kingside as expected.

White then played Nd2, developing his second knight. Black responded with c6, making moves like Qb6 and b5 possible.

The game resulted in a draw after 28 moves.

The English Opening: Symmetrical Variation

This opening gets its name from English master Howard Staunton, who played it in 1843.

White plays c4 to open the game. Black responds with c5.

White then plays Nf3, developing his knight and black responds with Nf6, also developing his knight. This is called the symmetrical variation of the English opening.

White can continue by developing his other knight with Nc3, to which black could respond with b6.

Advantages (for White):

- Helps White fight for the center early by gaining control of D5.

- Can lead to continued pressure on the Queen's side.

Disadvantages (for White):

- Slower development of White's pieces.

- Example: Wolfgang Uhlmann vs. Ljubomir Ljubojevic, 1973.

This game was played in Madrid, Spain, in 1973. Uhlmann had White pieces, and Ljubojevic had Black pieces.

To defend his e4 pawn, white played f3. This move also opened a door for white to develop his light-squared bishop. Black responded with e6, preparing to develop his dark-squared bishop.

White then played Be2, developing his light-squared bishop as expected. Black played Be7, developing his dark-squared bishop. In this position, both white and black are ready to castle kingside.

As expected, they both castled kingside.

White (Uhlmann) opened the game by playing c4. Black (Ljubojevic) played c5.

White continued with Nf3, developing his knight. Black played Nf6, also developing his knight.

White then played Nc3, developing his second knight. Black responded with b6, preparing to fianchetto his light-squared bishop.

Uhlmann won the game in 39 moves.

The King's Indian Attack

Although this move is rarely played at the highest levels, it is often played at club and amateur levels as it is easier to learn than other openings.

White plays g3 to open the game preparing to fianchetto his light-squared bishop. Black responds with d5.

White then plays Bg2, fianchettoing his light-squared bishop. Black responds with c6, defending his d5 pawn.

White continues with Nf3, developing his knight and black responds with Bg4, attacking white's knight.

Advantages (for White):

- May lead to a good attack on the King's side.

Disadvantages (for White):

- Allows Black to take control of the center of the board.

- Allows Black numerous options for defending.

- Does not put immediate pressure on Black.

- Example: Elizbar Ubilava vs. Bukhuti Gurgenidze, 1971.

This game was played in Tbilisi, Georgia, in 1971. Ubilava had White pieces, and Gurgenidze had Black pieces.

White (Ubilava) opened the game by playing g3, preparing to fianchetto his light-squared bishop. Black (Gurgenidze) played d5.

White played Bg2, fianchettoing his light-squared bishop as expected and preparing to castle kingside. Black played d6, defending his d5 pawn from future attacks.

White continued with Nf3, developing his knight and preparing to castle kingside. Black played Bg4, developing his bishop and attacking white's knight.

White then played c4, attacking white's d5 pawn and sacrificing his c pawn. Black could have accepted the sacrifice and captured white's c4 pawn, but that would have doubled his pawns on the c file. So instead, black played e6, opening a door to develop his dark-squared bishop. This also adds a defender to black's d5 pawn.

White played b3, adding a defender to his c4 pawn and preparing to fianchetto his dark-squared bishop. Black responded with Nd7, developing his second knight.

White played Bb2, fianchettoing his dark-squared bishop. Black played Nf6, developing his second knight.

25

White finally castled kingside as planned a few moves prior. Black played Be7, developing his dark-squared bishop and preparing to castle.	White played d4 to prevent black from playing Ne5. Black decided to trade his light-squared bishop for black's f3 knight and played Bxf3.	Naturally, white played Bxf3, recapturing black's light-squared bishop. In this position, black lost a bishop and white has a bishop pair.

Ubilava won the game in 40 moves.

The Hungarian Opening

This opening was first recorded in 1928.

White plays g3 to open the game, preparing to fianchetto his light-squared bishop. Black responds with e5.	White then plays Bg2, fianchettoing his light-squared bishop. Black responds with Nc6, developing his knight.	White then plays c4 and black responds with f5 to gain space on the board.

Advantages (for White):

- May lead to pressure on the Queen's side.

Disadvantages (for White):

- Gives White no control over the E5 square.

- Example: Vladimir A. Savon vs. Ratmir D. Kholmov, 1972

This game was played in Baku, Azerbaijan, in 1972. Savon had White pieces and Kholmov had Black pieces.

White (Savon) opened the game by playing g3, preparing to fianchetto his light-squared bishop. Black (Kholmov) played e5.

White played Bg2, fianchettoing his light-squared bishop as planned. Black responded with Nc6, developing his knight and defending his e5 pawn.

White continued with c4 and black played f5, gaining space on the board.

White then played Nc3, developing his knight. Black responded with Nf6, developing his second knight.

White then played e3, freeing the e2 square for his knight. Black played g6, preparing to fianchetto his dark-squared bishop.

White played Ne2 as planned. Black then played Bg7, fianchettoing his dark-squared bishop as expected.

27

White then played d3, fighting for the control of the center and preparing to play e4. Black played d6, preparing to develop his light-squared bishop.

White continued with Rb1, preparing to push his b2 pawn and attack black's c6 knight. White played Be6, developing his light-squared bishop.

White played b4, pushing his b pawn as planned and preparing to attack black's c6 knight.

Savon won the game in 39 moves.

The Nimzowitsch-Larsen Attack

This opening is named after grandmaster Bent Larsen.

White plays b3 to open the game, preparing to fianchetto his dark-squared bishop. Black responds with e5.

White then plays Bb2 as planned, fianchettoing his dark-squared bishop. Black responds with c5.

White continues with e3, opening a door for his light-squared bishop to join the center of the board. Black responds with Nf6, developing his knight.

Advantages (for White):

- Unusual opening that can be difficult to defend against.

28

Disadvantages (for White):

- Slower development on the King's side.

- Sometimes shuts White's dark-squared Bishop out of the game.

- Example: Bent Larsen vs. Han-Hein Donner, 1971.

This game was played in Madrid, Spain, in 1971. Larsen had White pieces and Donner had Black pieces.

White (Larsen) opened the game by playing b3, preparing to fianchetto his dark-squared bishop. Black (Donner) played d5.

White continued with Bb2, fianchettoing his dark-squared bishop as planned. Black responded with c5, gaining space on the board.

White then played e3, preparing to develop his light-squared bishop. Black played Nf6, developing his knight.

White played Nf3, also developing his knight. Black played g6, preparing to fianchetto his dark-squared bishop.

White continued with Bb5, developing his bishop and putting black's king in check. This move also prepares white for kingside castling. Black responded with Bd7, taking his king out of check and attacking white's light-squared bishop. In this position, white has the option to exchange light-squared bishops by playing Bxd7.

Instead, white chose to play Qe2, defending his light-squared bishop on b5. In this position, if black plays Bxb5, white will follow up with Qxb5, which would put black's king in check again. So instead, black played Bg7, fianchettoing his dark-squared bishop as planned and preparing to castle kingside.

White decided to exchange light-squared bishops and played Bxd7. Back recaptured white's bishop by playing Nxd7, developing his second knight.

White then played c4, attacking black's d5 pawn. Black castled kingside as planned.

White also castled kingside, to which black responded with Rc8. Black intends to open the c file in future moves and wants to take control of that open file with his rook.

The game resulted in a draw after 56 moves.

Catalan Opening

1.	d4	Nf6
2.	c4	e6
3.	g3	

Though Catalonia is politically part of Spain, the region retains its own language and a strong identity. Over the centuries, the territory has been violently fought over and has been the scene of many tragic massacres. It has been an independent state, ruled by Spain, and ruled by France. As a result, the Catalan language includes elements of both Spanish and French.

The Catalan Opening received its name from a 1929 Chess tournament held in Barcelona, the capital of Catalonia. To commemorate the event, the tournament organizers held a competition to name an original opening in its honor. The winner of this invent-an-opening contest was Savielly Tartakower, who was participating in the tournament (finishing 2nd, behind José Raúl Capablanca). Tartakower submitted the above sequence and took home the prize.

Despite its contrived invention, the Catalan Opening remains very popular today. It is a highly elastic opening where White focuses on attacking Black's queenside with the fianchetto light-square bishop.

Just a few years later, in 1936, the Spanish Civil War erupted. Catalonia fought on the side of the Republicans against the Nationalists of General Franco, who were supported by fascist Germany and Italy. Three years of bloodshed resulted in a crushing defeat for the Republicans and harsh reprisals for those who had fought on their side. The Catalan language was banned by the new Francoist dictatorship until 1975.

These days, Barcelona is a prosperous, cosmopolitan city. Nonetheless, the issue of rule from Madrid is still a hot topic. Catalan independence protests draw hundreds of thousands of impassioned supporters waving their distinctive red and yellow flags. The prospect of breaking away to form their own country has been consistently dismissed by the Spanish central government, but calls remain.

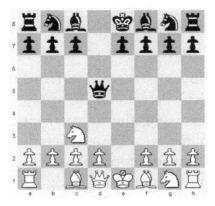

Position after 3. NC3.

The website chessgames.com features a vast database of recorded chess games going back hundreds of years. The very oldest game they have on record is a Scandinavian Defense, played in Valencia, Spain, in 1475. To put that in historical context, the game in question took place before Christopher Columbus had sailed to America!

The Scandinavian Defense gained its name mainly thanks to Ludvig Collijn, who served as chairman of the Swedish Chess Federation from 1917 to 1939. In his earlier days, Collijn competed at the 1897 Nordic Chess championship where, as Black, he responded consistently to 1. E4 with 1. D5. Collijn finished a respectable eighth in the tournament, which was incidentally won by a man called Sven Otto Svensson, which is quite possibly the most Swedish name imaginable.

But how did it come to pass that the tournament that gave the opening its name was the Nordic chess championship, yet Scandinavian was bestowed on it? It's the manifestation of an extremely common error; people often conflate "Scandinavian" and "Nordic" with each other, but in fact, they are not the same. The term "Scandinavia" includes the three kingdoms of Denmark, Norway, and Sweden. The languages of these countries retain enough similarities that Danes, Swedes, and Norwegians all understand one another to this day. Often, outsiders mistakenly include Finns and Icelanders when referring to Scandinavians, but strictly speaking, Iceland and Finland are Nordic countries, but not Scandinavian. Finnish and Icelandic people find Scandinavian tongues incomprehensible, and as Michael Booth joked in The Almost Nearly Perfect People, at Nordic Council meetings, the Finns and Icelanders tend to be found in a corner away from everyone else, speaking in English to one another.

The best player Scandinavia has ever produced is the 21st-century world champion Magnus Carlsen of Norway. He was a grandmaster at 13. At the same age, he managed to draw a rapid game against Garry Kasparov, the world number one at the time — a sensational result for someone so young. Carlsen continued to improve as he moved into adulthood, and he captured the coveted world crown from Vishy Anand in 2013.

In an era where computers reign supreme over elite human players, Carlsen plays the most like a machine out of anyone without a silicon brain. He thrives in the long-term strategy of the middle-game and is unbelievably tenacious in the endgame. Like a computer, he seemingly doesn't make mistakes once most of the pieces are off the board.

Carlsen doesn't play the Scandinavian Defense often — he is very much a modern Scandinavian, with no taste for flesh and blood of his Viking ancestors or the double-edged positions this opening is known for. He even supplements his chess earnings through fashion modeling.

Scandinavian Defense

1. e4   d5

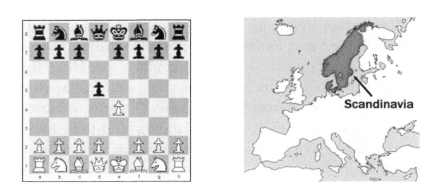

Scandinavia

In the French Defense, Black plays 1. E6, preparing 2. D5, and in the Caro-Kann Defense, Black plays 1. C6, again to support A 2. D5 surge. In the Scandinavian Defense, Black doesn't bother with any such groundwork and simply thrusts forward by playing 1. D5 immediately.

Modern Scandinavians are held up as exemplars of civilization. On the whole, they are blond-haired, IKEA-shopping, egalitarian, politically progressive people. This belies their history, for they are descended from the bloodthirsty Vikings, who made their name by pillaging and terrorizing northern Europe during the Dark Ages. The Vikings would go forth in their fearsome longboats, set ashore, and once they had their fill of plunder, return to their frigid homeland and drink from the skulls of their victims.

The Scandinavian Defense echoes the Scandinavian's vicious past far more than their mild-mannered present. It is a combative opening where the ill-prepared opponent can quickly be vanquished, just like the unsuspecting villagers set upon by the Vikings in days of yore. In the mainline, White captures the offered Pawn with 2. EXD5, Black wastes no time in recapturing with 2. QXD5, and White gains a tempo by bringing out his Knight and threatening the Queen: 3. NC3. All of this is expected by the prepared Scandinavian player. It is immediate hand-to-hand warfare.

Baltic Opening

1. Nc3

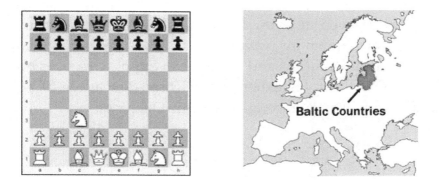

Baltic Countries

The Baltic Opening is a flexible first move. Since White will often play a knight to C3 early in the game anyway, it waits to see what Black does before committing a Pawn (which cannot be taken back). It develops a Knight to a central square, so it can't be considered a terrible move.

Whatever you call it, the main drawback of 1. NC3 is that it doesn't prevent Black from occupying the center of the board however he likes. 1. NF3 prevents 1. E5, but playing 1. NC3 does not prevent 1. D5 because the D5 pawn is protected by Black's queen.

The "Baltics" refer to the three countries in Northern Europe on the eastern coast of the Baltic Sea: Estonia, Lithuania, and Latvia. They were part of the Soviet Union until its dissolution in 1991, but today are members of NATO and the European Union. These Baltic countries had been invaded many times over the years, even before the most recent Soviet occupation, including by Sweden and by Germany. As a result, they have elements of Nordic, German and Russian culture in their food, architecture, and culture.

Arved Heinrichsen, a Lithuanian from the late 19th century, is responsible for the Baltic Opening's name. He traveled from his hometown of Vilnius to Berlin to study medicine, played at a few tournaments while in Germany, and became known for playing 1. NC3. Alas, the young man contracted tuberculosis and was sent to Egypt to recover but picked up malaria while there. Heinrichsen died at age 20, but his memory lives on through the Baltic Opening.

Paris Opening

1. Nh3

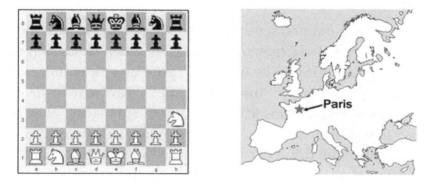

In the Paris Opening, White's kingside Knight hops from its starting square to the edge of the board, where it is seriously misplaced. The opening is flamboyant, garish, and outlandish, much like the Parisians themselves.

The opening got its name thanks to one of Paris's resident amateurs, Charles Amar. In fact, 1. NH3 is sometimes known as "The Amar Opening." Amar was not a particularly notable player, but he was shrewd enough to play 1. NH3 against an opponent who most certainly was—Savielly Tartakower. Tartakower was one of the highest-profile grandmasters of the 1920s and 1930s, and although he never became the world champion, he always gave a good account of himself against the very best. Tartakower was most notable for his authorship and sharp wit. A few Tartakower-isms will give you a flavor of the man:

"The blunders are all there on the board, waiting to be made."

"No game was ever won by resigning."

"A game of Chess has three phases: the openings, where you hope you stand better; the middle-game, where you think you stand better; and the ending, where you know you stand to lose."

Tartakower penned several famous books and contributed to widely circulated Chess magazines. So, when Amar played 1. NH3 against him while in Paris, Tartakower's wide reach was enough to make the name stick. Tartakower even adopted the move himself a few times. This story goes to show that there is more than one way to attain Chess immortality. You don't need to become the best player in the world to get an opening named after you if you can discover an offbeat opening with no name yet and get someone more well-known to notice.

Paris has a far more central place in Chess history than the opening that bears its name. The city was an intellectual hub during the Enlightenment; artists, musicians, and writers flocked there to be among one another and participate in the discourse. This new class of professional thinkers needed a meeting place, and in Paris, the place to be was the Café de la Régence.

The Régence was one of the famous coffee houses which had sprung up all over Europe from the 17th century onward. It has even been argued that the arrival of coffee was a contributing factor to the Enlightenment taking root in the first place. Instead of drinking themselves into a stupor with alcohol, people started to turn to mind-sharpening coffee.

The Régence became an important center for Chess, hosting many strong tournaments of Europe's best players. Many of the central figures of the Chess world played there at the height of its glory, including François-André Danican Philidor, Howard Staunton, Adolf Anderssen, and Paul Morphy. Great philosophers and statesmen also frequented the venue, including Benjamin Franklin, Karl Marx, Napoleon Bonaparte, and Voltaire.

Picture the scene in the Café de la Régence as coffee was supped, men smoked their pipes, ideas were exchanged, and Chess provided the entertainment for the casual players and the battleground for the serious ones.

By the time Charles Amar played 1. NH3 in the early 20th century, the coffeehouses were no longer hosting much Chess. And because of him, Paris, one of the most significant cities in the history of chess, surrendered its name to one of the game's least important openings. C'est la vie.

The King's Indian Defense

The King's Indian Attack is one of the most common Hypermodern opening techniques for the Light-coloured King player. The alternate or reverse of this opening is the King's Indian Defence, which is an opening for the Solid's. This opening is also known as the Barcza System.

The sequence of movements to be followed by both the players are:

- NF3 D5 (the White advancing through the flank while the Black advances its Knight)

- G3 NF6

- BG2 C5

- D3 NC6

- NBD2 E6

- BE7

- E4

This is one of the most strategic movements that any player will ever encounter. The Bishop light-squared Bishop is advanced and placed in position G2. This is done to cover the King. Having moved the King to a position of absolute safety, the White now fiercely open attacks on the Solid.

This technique is very smart yet simple. It uses the simple logic of advancing the Pawn and then opening an attack from the kingside. This elegant technique, due to the simple logic and understanding, is one of the most popular opening movements that is played in all levels of matches.

Alekhine's Defense

Alekhine's Defense is among the popular hypermodern opening techniques. It is equipped against the E4 play by the White. The sequence of movements can be summed as:

E4 movement by the White. The Pawn at the E2 square is moved forward by two blocks in the forward direction and is positioned at square E4

In counter to this movement, the Solids try to advance through the flanks, and instead of mirroring the movement of the White, it moves its Knight on the D file (the kingside Knight). Its counter-movement is therefore 1. NF6

As evident from the moment, the Solid is allowing the White to gain control of the center. Meanwhile, it delays its advancement to the center. It maintains a tempo and causes the White to chase around its kingside Knight throughout the board.

The proper timing and strategy are very important here, as the Solid now needs to attack the White rapidly. The attack by the knight needs to be sudden and quick. Else the Solid kingdom will crumble under the pressure that the White is capable of exerting on them after completely gaining control of the center.

After delaying the attack for a calculated amount of time, the Solid now has to be hostile and remove the pieces of the White King's kingdom almost instantaneously, within minimum counter moves. To this attack by the Solid, the White can choose to counter-attack the Solid's aggressively or play a gambit.

Whereas the Solid having control of the center through the flanks has the choice of wither getting more hostile or choosing simpler ways by removing the pawn of the Kingside of the White (the C file Pawn). Depending on the choices made by both the players, there can be various variations to the game with several choices of transposition too.

This opening can be very risky, and defeat becomes unfathomable once the Solid miscalculates the tempo or the timing gets on the wrong track. The White already solidifies its hold on the center, and thus, if the pieces do not get removed at the correct times, they will create high pressure on the Solid and make the kingdom crumble under pressure.

The grandmasters mastered the opening techniques, but unfortunately, they are not popular to the day anymore. However, there are some remarkable matches where grandmasters used the Alekhine Defence technique. Some of the most remarkable matches are:

- The match between H Borochow and Fine in 1932.

- The remarkable match was held in the year 1926 between grandmaster Nimzoqitsch. and Alekhine. This is one of the best examples to learn this technique in more detail.

- The 1935 match that was held between NN and Getachew.

- The 1925 match that was held between G. A. Thomas and Alekhine.

- The technique of Alekhine Defense always brought in victory in all the major tournaments except one.

Grunfeld Defense

Another hyper-modern technique for Solid's play is the Grunfeld Defense. This opening is having three main lines but is still a very risky approach. It is risky as the Solid lets the White have complete control of the center; hence the player needs to be extremely aware of the environment.

The sequence of movements involved in this opening technique is as follows:

- D4 NF6

- C4 G6

- NC3 D5

As evident from the movements, the Solid is in no hurry to gain any kind of control on the center. Instead, it threatens the White with a pawn on D4. By this time, the White is already in control of the space of the center and can use it to its advantage to leash attack on the Solid.

But here, the twist occurs. The White cannot exploit the spatial advantage it has as the D4 Pawn is directly threatening the Whites. It comes as a surprise element, and the White is bound to play on defense and try to counter the threat from the D4 Pawn.

This is yet another elegant technique of gameplay that can prove to be a lethal weapon in the correct hands. The surprise factor in the technique is making it an absolute favorite among many grandmasters. Although due to the high risks, it is still not very common among younger players. The risk is really difficult to cope with as one wrong move will cost the entire match within a handful of moves.

Some of the popular games where the grandmasters employed the technique of Grunfeld Defence are:

- The infamous game between two of the elite players, Fine and Drake in the year 1933.

- Drake again employed the Hypermodern opening technique of Grunfeld Defense in the year 1949 in a game against J Schmitt.

- The most recent and infamous game held between Kramnik and Shirov in the year 1998.

The game held between Alekhine and Bogoljubov is among the oldest games that employed Grunfeld Defense. It was played in 1929.

CHAPTER 4

Other Openings

Caro-Kann Defense

T his is a strong semi-open response to 1. E4. It may not be as dynamic as a few of the other options for Black against E4, but the ideas and plans are relatively easy to understand, which makes it a successful and widely used defense. The opening moves start with 1. E4 C6.

In most games, using the Caro-Kann technique, White usually replies with 2 D4, after which Black responds with D5. The Black attacks the Pawn on E4 directly, just like in the French defense, by exerting pressure on the 2nd move. Several options are now available for White.

White can decide to trade; it turns out to be a complex recreation wherein many competitions spend productive time Pawns with 3. EX D5 immediately, just like in the French defense. White opts to keep on playing in a similar fashion as in the French Exchange, like responding with 4. BD3. A relatively equal game can ensue, but it is usually less symmetrical when compared to the French. Back's C Pawn is missing, as opposed to the E Pawn.

When White decides to make an early trade in the Caro Kann defense, it may be accompanied by more ambitious aims.

4. C4, or the Panov Botvinnik Attack, leads to a Pawn formation similar to the one associated with the Queen's Gambit and can also invert into several lines visible after 1. D4.

White can also decide to play 3. E5 in order to avoid trades. Black will then counter with BF5, from which White will have several available moves, like BE3, NC3, and NF3.

However, White will typically decide to develop a Knight in order to defend the E4 Pawn. You can achieve this using either ND2 or NC3. These two moves have subtle differences on the sidelines, but there is no difference against the popular response by Black.

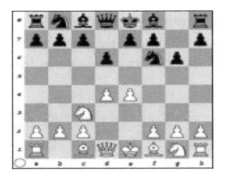

When Black responds to the development of the White Knight, either to C3 or D2, by capturing the Pawn on E4, White will usually play 4. NXE 4, resulting in Caro-Kann's Classical Variation. Black will have several options, with the most popular ones being ND7 and BF5.

The Pirc Defense

This opening is a hyper-modern defense, which means that it does not attempt to control the center of the board early on. Rather, Black attempts to attack the center from the sides using minor pieces. Once the foundation has been set, he then tries to weaken the center control, which is usually owned by

White. White has two main attacks to play against Black in the Pirc defense.

The most aggressive one is the Australian attack, with White pushing the F Pawn to F4, thus putting additional pressure on Black's King but exposing his King slightly in the process. In the Pirc defense, Black goes on to castle his King early on in the game, putting him on the side of a diagonal panel Bishop. It is usually a good idea to attack the King aggressively when this happens.

The Classical System is the second option that White has. It involves playing the 2nd Knight on F3 and aims to establish a stable center control before attacking. Black will have a counter-attack in both cases but has to be careful when playing this way. If he is not careful, Black can find himself in plenty of danger and a crowded position for him to move. If he attacks the center, he will have a great play before White gets the chance to attack.

The most common sequence after opening is E4 D6, D4 NF6, NC3 G6.

The Queen's Gambit

This is one of the most common openings known out there. One of the main reasons why many top players use it is that it is not really a Gambit because White loses a piece in the second move that can be won back. The goal with this opening is to maintain control over the center, but it can also lead into a devastating trap for Black. The starting sequence for the Queen's Gambit is:

- D4 for White Pawn

- D5 for Black Pawn

- C4 for White Pawn

The board ends up looking like this:

If Black accepts the move and responds with D5/C4:

The Black Pawn can now be trapped by moving the White Pawn to E3, using the Bishop to attack the Pawn. If Black plays C3 with his Pawn, the White Pawn can capture it.

Sometimes, Black can decide to play a Pawn to B5 in a bid to defend his Pawn. White will then respond with a move to A4, after which Black will counter by moving his Pawn to C6. This leads to a trap in the Queen's Gambit.

When White captures the Pawn at B5, and Black recaptures the position, White is left to make a devastating move, moving the Queen to F3.

The only move Black can make in order to save his Rook at A8 is to move his Knight to B6. This leaves White to capture at F3/B6 and establish a good position to dominate the game.

Colle System

This opening strategy, which can also be called the Colle-Koltanowski system, was formulated by Edgar Colle during the 1920s and was improved by George Koltanowski.

The Colle System stemmed from the Queen Pawn opening and features the following moves (ignoring the moves of the opponent):

- Move Queen's Pawn to D4.

- Kingside Knight moves to F3.

- King's Pawn to E3.

- Bishop on B1 moves to D3.

- Kingside castle.

- Castled rook moves to E1.

- C Pawn moves to C3.

- Queenside Knight moves to D2.

- A Pawn in E3 moves to E4.

This image will help you to visualize what the board should look like when using the Colle System (before the Pawn in E3 is moved to E4):

The order of the movements can be interchanged, as long as all pieces should be in place within 9 moves. The Colle System allows for a good way to develop your minor pieces (the Knight and the Bishop), gain some control of the center with the D4 Pawn and a threat from the F3 Horse on any piece that will occupy E5, open paths for your non-Pawn pieces (especially the Queen), and move the King away from the center as early as possible.

London System

This opening system was named as such because it was mostly used during the 1922 tournament in London. This system makes use of the Queen's Pawn opening but does not combine it with the Queen's Gambit (which is a common opening move). The system shares similarities with the Reti system since it also develops the Knight early on, followed by the Queenside Bishop. The variations of this system depend on the move of Black. However, if Black's movements are ignored, this opening system can be applied by making the following moves:

- Advance Queen's Pawn to D4

- Knight in G1 moves to F3

- Queenside Bishop moves to F4

This image shows what the board looks like if the system was successfully used:

The use of the London System presents early advantages on the side of White. First would be the obvious advantage of using the Queen's Pawn opening, which leads to automatic protection to one of your Pawns. Another is that the second and third move easily develops your kingside Knight and queenside Bishop, allowing you to check on other pieces that Black would want to develop, making the opening system also usable by those who are looking to attack. The Pawns on C2 and E2 can also be advanced one square as the game progresses, allowing you to bolster your defense in the center and protect the King (aside from castling) while giving you room to develop your remaining minor pieces and the Queen.

Stonewall Attack

To prevent your opponent from getting to your King, you will need to provide a good defense. If you are interested in a defense-based game plan, what you need is the Stonewall attack opening.

This system also uses the Queen's Pawn opening and doesn't use the Queen's Gambit, but along with the Queen's Pawn, this system involves moving the other Pawns in the center in such a way that they are protected either by other Pawns or the minor pieces. The Pawn's position in the center also allows for open lanes so that White can also guard any attacks from the flank.

To execute this opening, the following moves must be followed:

- Queen's Pawn to D4

- King's Pawn to E3

- Kingside Bishop to D3

- C Pawn to C3

- F Pawn to F4

If the moves are followed properly, the board must look like this:

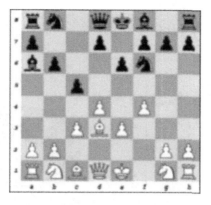

The use of the Stonewall attack allows White to guard whatever reaches the center square with its Pawns, allowing it to capture opponent pieces that will attempt to occupy the said area and provide the pieces with enough protection. This makes it difficult for Black to penetrate White with a direct approach. Unfortunately, flank attacks are also checked by White's long-range pieces, and even if Black does manage to start an attack on the King's side, it can easily be shut close by the Pawns in columns G and H.

Ruy López

1. e4   e5
2. Nf3   Nc6
3. Bb5

Ruy López was a priest from Spain who lived back in the 16th century. Some of the oldest recorded games are attributed to López and his frequent sparring partner, Giovanni Leonardo Di Bona, from Italy. Think of this, every time you sit down to play–through Chess, you share a bond with those like López who lived hundreds of years ago.

If you write your moves down, as yet unborn people will be able to replay your games long after you are gone and marvel at your brilliance (or lack thereof).

"Libro" contains some general strategic advice and a section on the historical origins of Chess.

It also includes the rules that were being used at the time, most of which are the same to this very day. Among the differences, "Libro" mentioned that a stalemate resulted in a win for the player, not stalemated rather than a draw.

A player could also win by capturing all his opponent's pieces, even if the enemy King remained uncheckmated.

If you have known the frustration of completely outplaying your opponent, only to have the game end drawn, you might wish that we could bring these old rules back.

López's book is the reason we call the above sequence of moves the "Ruy López." "Questo" (Damiano's older book) argued that after 1. E4 E5, 2. NF3, Black's best next move was 2. NC6. López disagreed with Damiano, arguing that 3. BB5 "refuted" 2. NC6. The claim was enough to affix López's name to the opening forevermore.

Today we know that 3. BB5 is certainly not a refutation of 2. NC6 and that the Ruy López opening is perfectly playable for Black. Bear in mind, "Libro" was written over 400 years ago, and López was blazing the trail of opening theory. We stand on the shoulders of our ancestors, and if we improve upon what they discovered, it shouldn't diminish their original achievement.

The Ruy López's opening (also known as the "Spanish Opening") has been studied endlessly in the intervening centuries. You could spend months and years delving into the various lines which the sharpest minds in Chess have pored over for all that time. Indeed, if you have any ambition to play Chess at the top level, this is exactly the sort of intensive study that will be required. The Ruy López's is one to avoid if you don't have much of an appetite for opening preparation, for you will quickly find yourself on the back foot if your opponent has crammed more theory into their head than you.

Later in life, Ruy López was elevated from the priesthood and became a Bishop of the religious kind, not the type found on a chessboard–although the mental image of this pious Spaniard moving around the cobblestones of his town exclusively diagonally is certainly an amusing one.

Sicilian Defense

e4c5

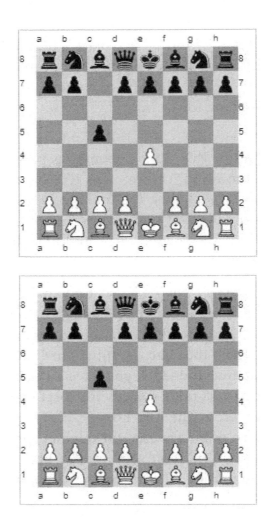

Easily the most popular and statistically successful opening for Black to the nearly universally played 1. E4 from White. While visually similar to the English Opening: Reverse Sicilian, this is a much older opening with a full and rich history. Indeed, enough has been said on the Sicilian to fill several books in their entirety with this opening alone. Let's start by analyzing the opening move from Black C4.

Just like in the Reverse Sicilian for White, Black aims to control the center of the board from a flanking wing Pawn, keeping their important D and E Pawns for a potential break in the middle later. Again, if Black could ever trade their C Pawn for White's d Pawn, he could see that as a slight advantage over White, as he could then have a central Pawn majority over the White player. As we have seen before, the advanced C Pawn also provides a great outpost for Black's Queen-side Knight that is a major factor in how the game usually plays out.

From a theoretical standpoint, Black is starting to lay a claim to the dark-colored squares in the center of the board. Imagine for a moment that Black could achieve their goal of a Knight on C6 as well as the eventual move E5. Notice the grip that Black would have on all those central dark squares. The C Pawn gives control over B4 and D4, the hypothetical Pawn on E5 targets the D4 and F4 dark squares, and a Knight on C6 could exert its influence on A5, B4, D4, and helps protect E5. This is a very common theme for Black to try and have a rock-solid grip on the dark squares, especially D4, where White would otherwise have plans of eventually making a break with moves like C3 and D4. Lastly, to further show dark-square dominance, a common strategy for Black will be to side panel their dark square Bishop at G7 giving them even greater control over those squares.

There are two mainline variations to the Sicilian Defense, called the Open and Closed Variations. Let's take a look at the Open Sicilian first:

Open Sicilian Defense

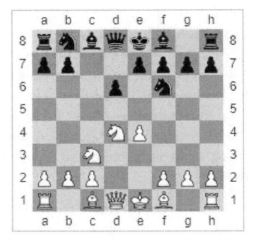

The main Open line goes as follows:

- E4C5

- NF3D6

- D4

White develops their King-side Knight, preparing to castle shortly. White is also taking a chance to control more of the center of the board, especially those dark squares we know Black is so keen on in D4 and E5. Black has other options for his second move other than D6; however, this is the most common reply. The move D6 by Black creates a Pawn chain with the c5 Pawn, solidifying the defense of that Pawn. Additionally, it opens a path for the light-square Bishop to activate along the C8–H3 diagonal. Finally, this move actually prepares Black to play their king-side Knight to f6. Notice how if Black played, the Knight move immediately, as in 2. NF3 NF6, White could cause some real problems for Black with the simple move: E5, threatening to capture our freshly developed Knight and taking a lot of central space. Best to avoid that scenario with the preparatory move D6.

From here, the main continuation is:

- D4CXD4

- NXD4NF6

- NC3

Black has achieved one of his goals of exchanging his C Pawn in for White's d Pawn. Black continues to develop the king-side Knight now that White can't disturb it with their E Pawn because of the D6 Pawn protecting the E5 square for us. White continues development with NC3.

In this position, Black will try to prove that his central Pawn majority is winning and has a clear advantage. White, on the other hand, has a significant lead in piece development, as well as more control over the center of the board, which he will argue, giving him more than fair compensation for his D Pawn.

Closed Sicilian

The mainline looks like this:

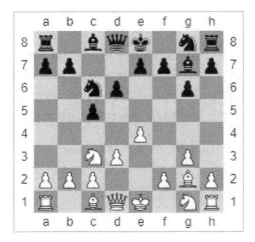

- E4C5

- NC3NC6

And here, Black will develop similarly to in the open Sicilian but not always in the same order. Black has goals they wish to accomplish and not a rigid plan of an attack requiring a strict move order.

We want that Knight on C6, and, usually, we want our Bishop to fianchetto on G7 (Notice how the Black Pawn chain is otherwise in the way for Black to put their Bishop on a meaningful square. Fianchetto is a great way to solve this problem!) We get our Queen-side Knight into the game on its favorite square now as well. This is a great example of why Knights like to be behind pawns.

Look at the difference between the two Knights on the C file. Notice how Black's C Pawn has contributed to his plan in a significant way. White would love to be able to play moves like C3 and D4 and grab some of that juicy center, but right now, his Knight on C3 is in the way! This is one of the major draws for players who enjoy playing flank openings such as the English and the Sicilian.

Let's see what is considered to be mainline, but again this move order can vary significantly:

- G3G6

- BG2BG7

- D3D6

Both White and Black have the same idea here: my Pawns are in the way, and I need to get my King-side Bishop into the game somehow. Once again, a fianchetto is an answer, and in this case, both sides will usually opt for this strategy, as they are both being walled in by their Pawn chain. White's Pawn on E4 is still on the way — for now. White can at any time open a discovered attack with a cheeky move like E5, both attacking Black's Pawn chain (assuming it is played after D6 from Black) and disrupting the scope of Black's Bishop. Both sides solidify their Pawn structure by creating Pawn chains in turn 5 with D3 and D6, respectively.

From here, both sides will develop their last pieces and castle, and we have reached a stable and about equal position to start a mid-game. Both sides have great chances here, and many fantastic positional games have been reached from this opening.

French Defense

E4 E6

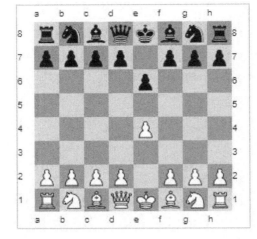

The French Defense is a fairly recent opening that began to see more prominent play in the early 1800s. This is a bit of a slower start compared to some of the more flashy openings and can lead to some very technically closed games.

The mainline opens as follows:

- E4E6

- D4D5

White gets his classical double pawn center, but Black intends to fight back from the very start with an early Pawn advance on D5 supported by his first move E6.

White has several responses. The most popular is 3. NC3 to protect the attacked E4 Pawn.

Another common try is 3. ND2 called the Tarrasch variation, which is similar to the usual move 3. NC3 in that it defends E4, but also different in the sense that the Knight has a broader scope for its second move, and the dark-squared Bishop has been blocked in, meaning it cannot be developed until a solution is created.

There is another variation known as the Advance Variation, where White plays 3. E5 taking the space given by Black's second move and avoiding the exchange of central Pawns.

Finally, there is the exchange variation that can be tried after 3. EXD5, which leads to a symmetrical Pawn structure, with each player having a Pawn on D4 and D5, respectively. The exchange variation leads to a position that is objectively equal for both sides, and either side will have to try to unbalance the position if they hope to achieve a win instead of a draw.

Winawer Variation

Let's take a look at 3. NC3 and a typical continuation of the mainline called the Winawer Variation now, as it is one of the well-studied continuations for the French Defense.

- NC3BB4

- E5C5

- A3BXC3+

- BXC3NE7

Let's walk through each move. White moves his Knight to C3, protecting the E4 Pawn. Black moves his Bishop to B4, creating a pin on the C3 Knight against the White King. This pin effectively means that E4 is no longer defended as that Knight cannot move to recapture while pinned to the King, as it would leave the King in check. An illegal move.

To deal with the undefended Pawn, White advances it to E5, claiming some extra space and making a Pawn chain with D4. Black seeks to undermine this Pawn chain with the Pawn move C5 attacking the D4 Pawn, protecting the E5 pawn now. White aims to dislodge the Bishop on B4 with the move A3 by attacking the Bishop with a lesser piece, making Black decide what they want to do.

Black captures the Knight on C3 and White recaptures with his B Pawn, creating doubled Pawns for White to worry about later. Finally, Black develops his King-side Knight to a square preparing to castle soon. White is still several moves away from being able to castle and if Black castles and breaks things open in the middle, White can find himself in a real danger being caught in the middle of the board with his King.

This variation is a very good try for Black to achieve equality or possibly an advantage. He is exchanging a slightly cramped space by virtue of White's E5 Pawn for a lead in development and better King safety.

Caro-Kann Defense

E4 C6

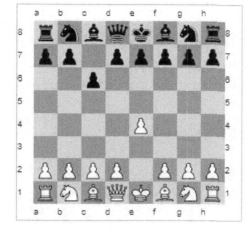

Compared to some of the big-name Chess openings like the King's Gambit and the Italian Game, the Caro-Kann Defense is a very newly adopted opening by Chess masters, only entering into professional play in the late 1800s.

From the initial position, White will almost universally play D4 to claim the classical D4 and E4 center White loves so much. Black's plan with C6 was to prepare for turn two and the move D5. Black immediately contests White for the middle. This tension makes many newer White players uneasy and results in an early exchange, which favors Black. Since if White is the one to initiate the exchange, Black will end up trading the C Pawn for White's precious E Pawn.

By preserving both central Pawns in the event of an exchange, Black hopes to avoid some potential weaknesses found in some other openings when playing for control of the center directly with a move like E5.

By creating this tension on D5 forces White to clarify his intentions and allows Black to react accordingly. There are three main ways White tends to reply, and these are the main variations of the Caro-Kann. They are the exchange variation, either of NC3 or ND2, as they very often transpose into each other, and the advanced variation where White pushes their Pawn to E5. The advance variation plays very similar to the French Defense, with some positional differences to consider.

Exchange Variation

This line starts out as follows:

- E4C6

- D4D5

- EXD5CXD5

Black strikes back into the center with D5, and White chooses to trade Pawns. The next moves vary, but the most common line and considered the mainline goes like this:

- BD3NC6

White develops their Bishop to D3. The main purpose of this move is to control the F5 square, preventing Black from developing to its light-squared Bishop to its optimal square on F5. The next moves can vary. But, to finish off the mainline for the exchange variation, a common continuation is:

- C3NF6

- BF4BG4

- QB3

White makes a solid Pawn chain with C3 and limits the potential scope of Black's dark-squared Bishop by taking away the B4 square. Black develops their King-side Knight to better defend the King-side squares, including G4, which will be important in a moment. White develops their dark-squared Bishop to a useful square on F4. And Blacks take advantage of the support of their Knight on F6 to play BG4 attacking White's Queen while developing to a useful square. Finally, White will move the Queen to safety and develop to a useful square by moving her to B3. This move gives her excellent scope over the board, including the now weak B7 Pawn, since the Black's light-color Bishop is now sitting on G4.

From this position, we have reached an equal position, with both sides having roughly equal chances.

Variations:

- NC3/ND2

This line is considered together since they will usually transpose into the same position after Black plays the move, 3. DXE4, and White is recapturing with the Knight at either position moving to be on E4. This is where the line begins:

- E4C6

- D4D5

- NC3/ND2DXE4

- NXE4

- The classical variation then continues:

- NXE4BF5

- NG3BG6

Black attacks White's undefended Knight after the capture, and so White retreats to G3 and now attacks the Bishop! The

Black Bishop retreats to G6 to stay in a good position and get out of harm's way.

There is actually a special relationship here between Black's Bishop and White's Knight that is pretty annoying for White to deal with. A Bishop that is 4 squares away from a Knight (e.g. BG6 and NG3) can cover every square the Knight can move forward.

Because of this reason, White will sometimes continue with the idea of eventually disrupting that Bishop with 6. H4. Black will usually respond with 6...H6 giving the Bishop a spot to back into if needed and stopping that H4 Pawn from disrupting Black's Pawn structure.

The mainline goes like so:

- H4H6

- NF3ND7

- H5BH7

- BD3BXD3

- QXD3

Both sides activate their Knights; Black wants to get into the action King-side, so it deploys to D7. White continues on with his Pawn on the h file, moving up a square. Black tucks his Bishop away in the corner where it will be safe as well as to shore up the space left behind by the move H6. White plays BD3—a final challenge to that pesky light-colored Bishop for Black: capture me or I will capture you and leave your King more exposed. Black is forced to trade Bishops, and White will collect the annoying Black Bishop once and for all with QXD3.

From here, we have a position where Black can hope to have some solid defensive options in the mid-game without having conceded too much to our opponent in terms of positional weakness.

The Nimzo's Indian Defense

This move follows 1. D4 NF6, followed by 2. C4 E6, then 3. NC3 BB4 sequence. This opening was developed and popularized by Aron Nimzowitsch.

He was one of the pioneers of the Hypermodern School of Chess. Hypermodernism was established in the early twentieth century and is based on the following counterintuitive notions:

1. The best way to control the center of the board is by using non-Pawn pieces.

2. You should encourage your opponent to establish a Pawn-dominance at the center. This formation will become vulnerable to attack once it has been overextended.

3. It is impossible to break down Chess into a simple set of principles; it is dynamic and fluid.

4. The Nimzo Indian opening is one of the most common hyper-modern openings. Black can maintain a flexible structure by not playing his Pawns at the center. This provides him with several counter-attacking opportunities. The B4 Bishop will usually be traded with the Knight it captures, leading to a multiplication of the C Pawns of White, a weakness.

The King's Indian Defense

The sequence of the King's Indian defense is:

1. D4 NF6

2. C4G6

3. BG7.

This opening was once regarded as unsafe, but soon gained fame and respect in the thirty's.

The King's Indian Defense is said to be riskier and more aggressive than the Nimzo Indian. The opening is extremely complicated and has been used by many top players extensively, including Fischer and Kasparov.

The center can be locked down in this opening, with Black having the advantage of kingside, while White gets the advantage of queenside. Interesting spectacles can follow, with Black aiming to infiltrate the King and White swooping down and tormenting the defenseless queenside.

CHAPTER 5

Basic Opening Strategies

Strategies allow you to play with greater confidence, being aware of what you have to do to gain a real advantage. During a Chess game, it is impossible to remember the various tactics and strategies because you have to think about many things: what is the opponent's plan, what are his weak points, what are my weak points, which piece should I exchange on which sector of the board is better to lead the attack, etc. In the middle of all these considerations, sometimes escape some tactics that we can perform. That's why you should always keep your eyes open to avoid missing something.

When you are on the chessboard for a while, it is difficult to remain as clear-headed as during the first moves. For this reason, some people advise you to step away from the board every 15 minutes to regain some awareness of what is actually happening on the board.

Keep Eyes Open

Watch your opponent's moves carefully. Which pieces is he developing, or which part of the board does he prefer? If you were in his shoes, what long-term strategy would you adopt? When you have learned the basics of the game, you should always adapt to the other player's moves. If he is defending himself, preparing the pieces on his side of the board for an attack, ask yourself what his ultimate goal is. Can you ruin his strategy or stop his plan? Does he have the advantage? Do you have to retreat and defend your most important pieces, or can you put him under pressure?

The Sacrifice

Learn when to eat by sacrificing one of your pieces. Swapping pieces is obviously the right choice when your piece is less valuable than your opponent's, for example, if you have to sacrifice a Knight to eat the enemy Queen, but deciding what to do is not easy when you have to swap Pawns of similar importance. In general, you should not sacrifice pieces when:

- You have an advantage in the position of the pieces, in controlling the center of the board, and in the development of the game. The fewer pieces in play, the smaller your advantage and the easier it is to defend against your attacks.

- Your opponent is trapped in a corner or obstructed by his own pieces. When you have your opponent cornered, it will be harder for him to move if he has many pieces, but he may be able to break free if he has fewer pieces.

- You have fewer pieces than your opponent. If you have more pieces than the other player and neither player has a clear advantage, start eating. You will open up new paths to attack.

- You would bring two Pawns in a row to each other. This makes those Pawns much less useful, clogging up your side of the board. However, if you forced an opponent to bring two Pawns in a row to make an exchange of pieces of equal value, you could use this situation to your advantage.

Always think 5–6 moves ahead. This is easier said than done, but you will need to have a long-term strategy to win Chess games regularly. You should move each piece with three objectives in mind. If you always consider these aspects, you will quickly improve your winning plans:

- Develop many pieces (Rooks, Knights, Queens, Bishops) in the early stages of the game and do so often. Move them from their starting squares to have more options available.

- Check the center. The center of the board is the most important area to dominate.

- Protect the King. You may have prepared the best attack in the world, but leaving the King undefended almost always leads to defeat.

Evaluate each move objectively. You should look at the whole board, considering all possible moves. Don't move a piece just because you have to: think about it and always look for the best move to make. The most effective choice depends purely on the context of the game, but there are some questions you can ask yourself to see if a move is the right one:

- Am I in a safer position than I was before?

- Am I exposing that piece, the King, or another important Pawn to attack?

- Can my opponent put my piece in danger, forcing me to go back and "lose" a turn?

- Does this move put pressure on my opponent and force him to react?

A Flawless Defense

Eliminate your opponent's pieces without isolating your Pawns. You must maintain control of the center of the board but attack in a compact manner. Pieces are like members of an orchestra: each has a unique purpose, but they are most useful when working together. By eliminating your opponent's pieces, you weaken his King's line of defense and, if you use two or three units to support your attack, you can advance without losing your material advantage.

79

Hold on to your advantage until you can make the most of it. Inertia is important in Chess, and when it is on your side, you must do everything not to lose it. If your opponent merely reacts to your moves, defends his pieces against your offensives, and does not counterattack, weaken him without rushing. Remember, you can win an exchange and still lose the game. Do not advance if it means exposing yourself to a counterattack. Instead, just eat the pieces your opponent uses to defend himself, gain total control of the center of the board, and only hit the enemy when you can make it really difficult.

Learn to block pieces. Blocking a piece means trapping it and preventing the opponent from using it unless he is willing to lose it. This 'passive' attack is great for controlling the game and will help you dominate your opponents. To execute it, study the possible moves of an enemy piece. Usually, Pawns that have movement restrictions are the easiest to attack. When you have finished your analysis, instead of going on the offensive, move one of your pieces so that it threatens all the squares that the opponent's piece can reach, effectively rendering it useless for some time. You can also block an opponent's piece by making it eat one of your own, but only by sacrificing yourself. The other player may or may not decide to eat it, but you are in control.

Always protect the Queen with a Bishop or Rook. There will rarely be occasions when it is worth sacrificing the most powerful piece on the board, even to capture the enemy Queen. Your Queen is the most versatile offensive piece, and you must use it accordingly. Always protect and support her because almost all players will sacrifice their pieces to capture her.

Queens can only reach their full potential if they have support. Almost all players instinctively observe their opponents' Queens, so use yours to force Pawns to move into spaces threatened by Bishops, Knights, and Rooks.

Don't hinder your Bishops with your Pawns. Those pieces can attack from a great distance, and using both to control the board is essential, especially in the early stages of the game. You can learn many opening strategies, but your overall goal will be to clear the way for the most important Pawns so they can move freely.

Moving Pawns to D4/D5 or E4/E5 clears the way for the Bishops and helps you take control of the center of the board. Free the Bishops early, then use their long-range to protect the Queen and Rook advances.

Fork Attack

This is the first attack strategy we will discuss. It is the double (or fork) attack.

Why does the image above depict Horses? Because these are the pieces par excellence specialized in this area. As the phrase itself implies, this strategy consists of attacking two (or more) pieces simultaneously with a single attack.

As an example, let's imagine a Black Rook on F4, another on B4. Now imagine that there is also a White Knight on D3... you have a double attack! The Knight attacks both Rooks at the same time, and Black will surely lose one of them. Obviously, the attacks can also be triple, quadruple, and so on. The beauty of these attacks is that, since they can only make one move at a time, the enemy can only defend one of the threatened pieces, and the others will be lost as a result.

Threading

I think this strategy is easier to do than to explain. First of all, let's say that if for the double attack, the best piece is the Knight, for the enfilade, the strongest piece is the Queen. This strategy consists of attacking an opponent's piece that is placed in the same line of action (column, crosspiece, diagonal) as another opponent's piece.

In practice, if we attack an opponent's Bishop with a Queen, and behind that Bishop, there is another Bishop, our opponent will still lose a piece because he will move the first Bishop, but the second will be captured.

Example: White: Queen F3 Black Bishop F5 and Bishop F8.

The White Queen threatens a Bishop, and the Bishop moves (to get out of the way of the attack) but offers another piece to the White Queen. This move can be saved, however, if you have these pieces White: Queen F3 Black pieces: Bishop F5, Bishop F8, and Pawn E7. Let's assume that White has moved, and now it's Black's turn to defend. How can he free himself from this entanglement? Just push the Pawn from E7 to E6 so that it defends and supports Bishop F5.

Nailing

Nailing could be said to be the reverse process of threading. Here again, the strongest piece is the Queen, but there is nothing to stop the Bishop and Rook from nailing. Nailing occurs when one's own piece attacks an opponent's piece, and the latter cannot move because it is defending its own King.

This is the case with:

White piece: Bishop C3. Black piece: Rook E5 and King H8.

The White Bishop threatens the Rook on E5, which cannot move because it is covering its king on h1. If the opponent moves the White Rook has the right to declare an "Illegal move" and depending on the tournament, the arbiter will take his own measures (which almost always consist in the loss of time on the opponent's clock or even loss of the game if we are in a lightning game or a semi-light game).

Checkmate of Discovery

And finally, we talk about checkmate, perhaps one of the strongest and most difficult attacks to see. This one is based on the check, but check by itself without a strategy is not very useful, and whoever plays against Fritz knows this; in fact, he often repeats: "he who checks without purpose regrets it sooner rather than later."

Therefore, it is better to checkmate only when we can checkmate by discovery. This happens when you move one of your pieces as if to checkmate the opponent's King, but you don't checkmate because there is one of your pieces between your piece and the opponent's King. As soon as you move this interposed piece, the opponent's King goes in check and is forced to defend against the check.

Example:

- White pieces: Rook G7, Bishop F6

- Black pieces: King H8, Queen E1.

If it is White's turn and he plays 1. T G1, the Black King is in check because of the Bishop! So Black is forced to defend against the check by moving, and White has all the time he wants to capture the Queen on E1.

How to Make Extraordinary Moves

There are Chess moves that seem to be invisible to our eyes, and yet they are there!

The difference between a professional athlete from any other field and an amateur is that the professional athlete has many more chances than an amateur, whereas, in Chess, he does not. Let me explain. A professional high jumper has a much better chance of succeeding in jumping a 1.50m high pole (indeed, he does it while sleeping...) than a beginner. He has an enviable athletic preparation, strengthened leg muscles, and much more.

A professional basketball player is much more likely to score a basket from 7 meters than an amateur. He has thousands of hours of training, infallible technique, and athletic preparation behind him. A professional pianist will be able to play 40 notes in 2 seconds while the amateur will not be able to, even with all the effort in the world. I could give you millions of examples.

In Chess, on the other hand, a professional and an amateur have (potentially) the exact same opportunities in the sense that the moves of the pieces are the same and everything is there on the board. Just as I can move the Knight, so can the world champion. He can't do things that I can't do.

So what makes the difference? Well, the professionals know what piece to move and when to move it. Watch this example with me:

The green arrow shows you the move that Spassky (former world champion) played in 1973. Black puts the Rook on D2, completely taken over by the White Queen on E2. But... wait!

The Queen can't eat that Rook! Because if the Queen captures the Rook, it follows... knight F3!!! Capturing the Bishop and making a double attack between the King and Queen. Wow! Now, these are the moves you need to start seeing in the game, and these are the moves that allow you to take advantage.

CHAPTER 6

Tactics to Support Strategies

Elements of Coin Strategy

W hat matters is not so much where the pieces are located as to where they can go — the number and strength of the squares they can move to.

In a game of Chess, the relative value or effective power of a piece depends on its location on the chessboard and its relations to other pieces, and not primarily on its theoretical value. At the end of the game, for example, a Pawn about to be promoted often becomes more valuable than a Rook.

The Rook and the Columns

A powerful Rook is a Rook that aims towards many squares. The simpler the game, the more freedom and power the Rooks acquire. The mobility and coordination of turns make it possible to exert mate threats and to support (or slow down) the advance of the Pawns.

A player will seek to occupy an empty column with a Rook as quickly as possible. Since two aligned Rooks support each other, it will be beneficial to make them communicate as quickly as possible; especially at the end of the game.

The Bishop and the Diagonals

A powerful Bishop is a Bishop who aims towards many squares.

The two central diagonals are particularly powerful since they are the longest. In addition, they pass through the center. The two ways to access these diagonals are to place a Bishop in the center or to put it in the side panel.

Bishops and the Occupation of the Great Diagonals

Each of the two camps controls a large diagonal. The Whites have put their Bishop in the side panel, while the Blacks have theirs in the center. Two options that can turn out to be equally good.

A Bishop always moves on squares of the same color. Hence the following remarks.

A Bishop who is on squares of the same color as the majority of its own Pawns is blocked by them. For this reason, it is called a "bad fool."

It is therefore important to place your pawns in such a way as to free up diagonals where the Bishops can move freely.

Two Bishops placed side by side or one above the other form a kind of wall that a King, for example, cannot cross.

The Bishop Wall

The coordination of the 2 White Bishops makes it possible to erect an impassable wall to the Black King.

Having the pair of Bishops is an important asset, especially when the game is particularly open, as is the case in the final.

The Knight and the Center

The knight is the only piece that can jump over the others. It is, therefore, very strong at the start and in the middle of the game when the Pawns are not yet advanced or when the center is blocked, but less in the final.

The closer a Knight is to the center, the more it controls a large number of squares and the more power it gains. Conversely, the further a Knight moves away from the center, the more its room for maneuver decreases, and the less powerful it is.

The Power of a Knight According to Its Position

In the center, a Knight controls 8 squares. At the strip, this number decreases to 3, and, in a corner, to 2. Placed at 1 Knight's distance from one another, two Knights from the same camp have the property of protecting each other, and therefore of replacing each other in the event of capture or exchange. A property that Bishops do not own.

To block a Knight, nothing better than a Pawn or a Bishop placed 3 squares in front of it.

It is useful to know that one of the boxes less accessible to the Knight is the one located 2 boxes from it diagonally; at least 4 hits are needed to access it, and therefore 3 to pose a threat.

How Can a Bishop "Tame" a Knight?

Posted in this way in front of it, the Black Bishop holds the White Knight in check. In addition, and without having to calculate the moves, Black knows that they do not have to fear a failure of a Knight, and therefore of a fork, before at least 3 moves.

The Queen and the Space

The Queen enjoys great mobility since she can control up to 27 squares at the same time.

For this reason, it will be coveted and will quickly become the target of opposing pieces if it ventures prematurely into the center or into enemy territory.

Also, the Queen must know at the same time to stay a little in the background (in order to protect her pieces while remaining under their protection), to keep an eye on the opposing camp (by threatening to enter it at any time), and only expose herself on the front line with the support of her troops.

We can keep this very simple rule for the start of the game: unless there is a major reason, never leave your Queen on a square where she could be threatened the next move by a piece less strong than her (usually a Pawn or a Knight).

The King and the End of the Game

At the start of the game, the King is a weak piece. And since the fate of the game depends on him, he should be protected, particularly thanks to castling.

At the end of the game, when long-range pieces are scarce, the King can become a strong piece, able, in some cases, to stand up to even a Rook.

It is therefore not necessary to delay too long in bringing him back to the center of the chessboard, from where he can slow down the advance of the opposing Pawns and support his own Pawns.

The Pawns and the Structure of the Pieces

A coin has little value in itself. Its value comes to it from its power of action, its position on the chessboard, the threats it can generate, the space it has to move around, and the relations of mutual protection that it maintains with other parts of its camp. As well say that its value evolves during the game.

Ideally, the pieces should both protect each other and not block each other.

Development

At the start of a game, Pawns block Bishops, Rooks, and Queens. Only Knights can go out. Being even more stuck than other rooms, Rooks will have to wait a long time before being activated.

The first moves to be played will therefore be Pawn moves (preferably those in the center or those which free the bishops), as well as Knight strikes. Then, will usually come Bishop or Queen blows, castling, and finally those of Rooks.

As a general rule, especially at the start of the game, it is not advisable to waste time playing the same piece several times in a row. In addition, each move should ideally allow the pursuit of several simultaneous objectives: develop or protect a part, control a key box, open a line, etc.

Battery Attack

When you think of Battery Attack, imagine a regular electric battery. Each battery is powered by electric cells. If you want more control, you have to acquire extra cells. In Chess, a battery attack is formed on the rows (ranks and files) by gathering Rooks and Queen, while, diagonally, a Bishop and a Queen are stacked. Unless this is done, the opponent wields more power.

Both the players can use different pieces in their Battery Attacks. However, assume the White battery includes 2 Rooks at the same time as the Black battery includes 2 Rooks and a Queen. Black has a stronger battery, and White is smart to consolidate his 2 Rooks and thus prevent an assault.

Block

The block is a shielding tactic and is used whenever a Bishop, a Rook, or an opposing Queen manages to govern their King. In such circumstances, you may try to wiggle through with the help of your Pawns or other pieces to the center of the opponent's attacking unit and the King-take a look at the Block and shield the King, at least temporarily.

Be aware, and even if your Block unit includes the King or other infantry or support devices, the attacker may determine to marvel at the blocker in a sacrificial maneuver that has been recorded to remove some of your King's defense.

Authorization

It is also called "easy cleaning," which better describes what's happening here. Imagine you need to establish your hold on a selected square to reinforce the assault you ride. The problem here is that one of your pieces is already in that square.

The issue right here is that transferring that piece ends in its recording. However, due to the superior function, you may get via getting the other piece in that square, it's miles-worth "clearing" that block of the piece, accepting its sacrifice, to compensate for the harm you need. If the answer to this is positive, you may decide to go ahead with the move.

CHAPTER 7

How to Use Chess Tactics Correctly

A good Chess player may seem to be natural, but a masterful one certainly has his or her share of tricks. Here are some tips and tricks you can use to improve your game:

Start off with the basics: Having the knowledge of the basic rules of Chess will surely help. If you know the basic movements of each piece, you will not be lost in strategy. Know the difference between the two types of Chess-variants (Chess with different pieces or playing areas) and Chess variants (rules that make it similar to a game of Chess but change the basic ideas). Familiarize yourself with the basic patterns of pieces, and if you have time, you can memorize some opening sequences.

Practice makes perfect: If you want to improve your game, practice is a must. You should start by playing against a weaker opponent who will let you win sometimes.

Get to know your opponent: Know how your opponent plays. Will he play aggressively? Will he defend until the end? Try to know their play style and plan ahead.

Prepare for the worst: Plan your strategy for each possible move. If you are going up against an aggressive opponent, make sure you have a plan if they take your piece. For example, if they take your Knight, do you have a plan to get it back, or are you lost?

Be quick: This is one of the most important tips and tricks in Chess. You should be able to think quickly and choose an appropriate move. If you have more time on your clock than your opponent, this gives you more room to make a mistake before it becomes too late. Keep an eye on the timer! Know when it's time to be patient, when it's time to go all out, and when it's time to apply pressure on the board by having many pieces in a line (a tactic called pushing).

Fight with your brain: If you want to learn more, start memorizing positions and lookup high-quality Chess videos online. Search for Chess literature and Chess books are written, or find out who are the best Chess players in the world. You can also improve your strategy by reading about their tactics in articles.

Be versatile: If you get a chance, join a Chess club where there are different players, and there is no rating system. It will help you learn many different moves every day. This way, you will not be stuck knowing only one type of opening moves (or one type of tactic). Find out what your play style is so that you can adapt it to fit the other player's style of playing while still improving your game overall.

Stretch yourself: If you are bored at home, try playing Chess outside. This will help you keep from getting bored and actually making progress in your game. Ask for help if you need anything, especially if you are new to the game.

Look for training games online: You may want to start by playing training games on Chess websites; it will help with your memorization of positions and opening moves as well as your thinking skills.

Get a mentor: A good mentor can help you improve your tactics and playstyle while also teaching you about the game of Chess (whether it be books, or articles, or videos). If you have someone who is willing to teach and guide you in the right direction, then, by all means, take them up on the offer! For an experienced player who can teach an absolute beginner how to play better? Then there's nothing more they could want from their student.

These tips might seem obvious to some people but could still be helpful for other people trying to improve their game. If you have any other advice, please write them in the comments, and I'll add them if I feel they are worthy of doing so.

Tips for Improving Chess Openings

The opening phase of a game of Chess forms a very important aspect of the game. It can not only provide a good start but can also determine the winner. In order to get good results, one has to have a good opening strategy irrespective of whether he or she is a grandmaster or a beginner. You can improve your opening knowledge with the help of a Chess coach. However, you can also do some self-study in order to improve your game.

Here are some tips with the help of which you can improve your chess openings:

Selecting Your Lines

Unless you have a Chess partner or a Chess coach, you might end up spending most of your time perfecting this area. A majority of players tend to pick the lines as per their own playing style. Therefore, you have to first figure out what your better qualities are, then choose an opening style that you think will help you and suit your style.

For instance, you should concentrate on making closed openings if you prefer strategic positions. On the other hand, you could go with sharp openings if you are comfortable in tactical chaos. It is recommended that you don't try to play everything at once. You should concentrate on 2 to 3 lines at first and try to master them properly.

Develop Your Pieces

Developing your pieces in the opening phase of a chess game refers to preparing them for battle by moving them out of their starting squares. To have the best chance of winning, you need all your pieces in play. You can't afford to lose even one move during the opening. If you are able to develop your pieces quicker than your opponent, you will have a lead in development. This will help you attack first.

It is often recommended that you move your Bishops and Knights before you move your Rooks and Queen. Your plan should be to castle early by developing the Bishop and Knight on the side. You should try to ensure that your Bishops and Knights are not at their starting positions even after the first ten moves.

Model Games

There are some opening lines that can be played in multiple ways since they are not so theoretically demanding. It is recommended that you search for important games played by professional players to get an idea about how to open strongly rather than trying to memorize all the possibilities and moves that you and your opponent can make. Once you get an idea, you can apply them in your own games. This strategy is probably one of the most helpful methods of understanding an opening.

Do Theoretical Research

You can start to learn the theoretical process once you have chosen your repertoire. You can do your research using an encyclopedia, books, or other such publications. Try to learn them by heart by studying them over the board multiple times. Knowing the theory well will give you more time to think about any difficulties that might arise during the game and also save time on the clock as you decide your opening moves.

Blitz Practice

A great way to study Chess opening strategies is by training with a partner. After you have completed your theoretical research, try playing out the lines using both White and Black. This will help you learn about the different tricks and subtleties present in the opening. You can play online if you don't have a training partner. You will feel more comfortable during a game if you have practiced the opening numerous times. Therefore, try to practice as much as you can. It will not only help you choose your opening strategy confidently but also help you to spot your opponent's strategy faster.

Look for the Specialists of the Lines

Search for professional players who use the line you have chosen and try to understand how they are playing their game regardless of the exact theoretical line. This will help you understand the possible situations, plans, and structures you might face when you are playing. A majority of strong professional players add a surprise factor to their games or avoid preparation by using different variations in a single opening. Studying their gameplay will also help you learn more ideas.

Prepare Your Own Opening Folder

Keep all the work you have done so far in an organized and dandy manner so that you can refer to them and review them any time you require, particularly before your game. You can create a folder and store all the model games and theoretical lines that you have selected in it. This way, all your work won't be in vain.

Keep an Open Mind

Strategies of chess openings keep on evolving. You might think that you have a good opening, but you might have problems with the same opening strategy the next time you play a game. This can happen to any Chess player, even professionals. Even books have to be rejected after a while. Therefore, it is important that you keep an open mind and flexible thinking. You should be willing to update your opening repertoire and make the required adjustments.

You need to be aware of any new ideas that your opponent could have developed and keep up to date with all the new game strategies. You can also use Chess engines. They can be a good tool to help you look for novelties, which you can then use to surprise your rivals. Try to find the critical areas in your opening strategy and build new ideas on your own. This will surely produce immediate results.

If your opening is bad, it can put an early end to your game. Your main aim when you study opening strategies should be to get to a playable position and have a clear idea of the way your pieces need to be developed and the strategies you need to follow in order to do it.

CONCLUSION

That's it! That's the book! I hope you gained a lot of insight into how to start your Chess games off on the right foot every time you play.

By having a solid opening strategy, you can set your opponent back on their heels and make them second-guess their own lines of attack and defense. This is so important to taking early control and keeping it. We also talked about some historically significant instances as examples of why starting off string is vital to increasing your chances of winning.

Openings are chess tactics introduced in the opening game to take control of the middle of the chessboard. The game-opening kicks off with the first move and ends when the middle board, usually after about ten moves each, and is dominated by one player.

Right in the middle of the chessboard, the center of the board consists of four squares. Regulation of the centerboard makes attacking and advancing pieces more challenging for your opponent. Therefore, a highly coveted tactical advantage is the possession of the centerboard.

Now that we have come to the end of the "Chess Opening for Beginners' guide," and maybe you have already tried other guides in the past, but you just could not find a suitable opening for you. This time will be different.

This game doesn't just provide strategic mental stimulation; it also has a long history dating back to before the 6th century. As a part of the social fabric of many cultures, it has stood the test of time, tying together humanity with a game of strategy.

You have to note that this is just an introduction to Chess. Every point we have presented to you up to this point are those we deem important to you as a beginner. There is no need to fill your head with more information that may end up leaving you more confused than you were before you picked up this to read.

Get yourself a chessboard and get familiar with all the components of the board. Try and memorize all the squares, ranks, and files. Once you are done doing that, the next thing you should do is to arrange the Chess pieces on the board correctly. Start by playing with yourself; you will need to play the White and Black pieces yourself. This is a great way to perfect a new skill you just learned. The more you practice with an actual chessboard, the more you will master how the different pieces move on the board. While playing, make sure you apply all the techniques you have learned. Make use of forks, pins, and the many other techniques we have talked about before.

However, when you are just starting, I would recommend that you shun online competitions entirely. You need to learn on your own first before engaging in competitions. Many mobile Chess games allow you to play with the system as your opponent, and that's one of the easiest ways to learn how to play Chess.

As you play more, you will grow inquisitive, and this is what will make you try to seek out more information on how to surmount a particular challenge you face.

So, pick out your favorite openings and read about them several times to make sure you fully understand the theory behind them and remember the sequence of moves that comprise them. Do not forget to put what you have learned to practice by playing games.

The next step is to start applying everything you learned here in real life. In order to be a good Chess player, you need to have the right knowledge about the openings and have a solid grasp of a variety of styles in which you can open your game. Play quick and blitz games to enhance your understanding of positions more. Another thing that will help you in becoming a better player is analyzing games from the database.

The game of Chess is an art. In fact, it is a form of thought. The player's mind is what moves the Chess pieces on the board. If the players have advanced Chess skills, they also can make their mind move the chess pieces and hence the game. Anyhow, the game of Chess is always a game of thinking, and spending some time on it allows the player to maintain their normal state of mind.

If any openings in this book seem strange or too difficult for you, don't start with those. Start with the easier ones, get used to them, and then move on to the difficult ones. In this way, you will not get overwhelmed and be able to learn something. And lastly, never underestimate your Chess opponent. The moment you start thinking that you are the best player in the room, you will start losing your focus and concentration and not be able to see where the blow came from.

Made in United States
North Haven, CT
12 November 2022